This book belongs to

_____

ALL ABOUT PEOPLE

A Bantam  BEGIN-TO-LEARN Book

BANTAM BOOKS

TORONTO · NEW YORK · LONDON · SYDNEY · AUCKLAND

ALL ABOUT PEOPLE

A Bantam Book / October 1985

PRINTING HISTORY

Adapted from the Walt Disney Fun-to-Learn Library:
All About You *(volume 11) and* People at Work *(volume 14).*

Library of Congress Catalog Card Number: 85-43075

ISBN 0-553-05536-4

Published simultaneously in the United States and Canada

Bantam Books are published by Bantam Books, Inc. Its trade-
mark, consisting of the words "Bantam Books" and the por-
trayal of a rooster, is Registered in U.S. Patent and Trademark
Office and in other countries. Marca Registrada. Bantam
Books, Inc., 666 Fifth Avenue, New York, New York 10103.

PRINTED IN THE UNITED STATES OF AMERICA

DW   0 9 8 7 6 5 4 3 2 1

ALL ABOUT YOU

Think about all of the things you do each day that keep you busy and make you happy. Did you know that even when you are asleep you are busy doing things? There is so much you can find out about yourself, and about how to take care of yourself, too. It's very exciting, learning all about *you*.

When you were born, you were a very little baby. You couldn't walk or talk or play or do any of the things that you do now. Think how much bigger you are, now that you have grown. All the time you are busy playing and learning, you are also growing. You will keep getting bigger and bigger until you are about 18 years old. After that you will stop getting taller, but you might still get fatter.

But you need something to keep you growing and playing and learning.

You need the food you eat. Food makes you grow, and it gives you energy. Energy helps you do things you want to do, like running and jumping and playing. Your body makes energy out of food. But you need good food—like meat and bread and vegetables and fruit and milk and cheese. Candy and cakes don't give you the right kind of energy to help you grow up strong and healthy.

When you eat, you chew the food with your teeth and break it into little pieces. Then you swallow, and the food goes down into your stomach. Your stomach digests it by squeezing it into tiny pieces. Once it is digested, the food that makes you grow and gives you energy goes to all the parts of your body.

Your bones hold up your body. All your bones together are called your skeleton. You have bones inside of your arms and legs and hands and feet. You have bones to protect the soft inside parts of you, like your heart and lungs.

Because your bones are hard, they can't bend. But there are places called joints where two bones meet, and luckily joints can bend. Your knees, elbows, ankles, wrists, and hips are joints.

Your muscles hold you together and help you move.
Muscles are like thick ropes attached to your bones. You
use your muscles when you move your arms or your legs.
When you want to bend your arm, your muscles get shorter
and bunch up. When you want to put your arm down
again, your muscles get longer—and down goes your arm.

Your heart is a muscle that is about the size of your closed fist. It squeezes hard and pushes your blood all through your body. Each time your heart squeezes, it makes a little thump inside your chest. You can feel it if you put your hand against your chest. This thump is called your heartbeat.

Your heart beats all the time, even when you are asleep. It usually beats 70 to 80 times a minute. But if you run very hard, it will beat faster.

You also breathe in and out all the time. When you breathe in, your lungs gulp in air. A part of this air is called oxygen. People must have oxygen to live.

Your lungs are like two bags inside your chest. When you breathe in, they fill up with air. The oxygen in the air passes through your lungs and is carried to every part of your body. When you breathe out, the part of the air your body doesn't need goes back out of your mouth and your nose.

Skin comes in many different colors, but everyone is some shade of brown—from very light brown to very dark brown. It depends on how much brown color, or pigment, you have in your skin. Freckles are little clumps of brown coloring.

Your skin is your outside covering. It's waterproof and it protects you from germs. If you get a cut, your skin makes a little scab to cover the cut while it is healing. Then germs can't get inside. A scab is your own homemade bandage.

Hair, too, comes in different colors. The thick hair on your head protects your head from the sun in the summer and the cold in the winter. Sometimes you need to wear a hat, as well.

Your hands are another very important part of you. Think of the many things you do with your hands. You paint pictures with your hands. You eat with your hands. You even count with your hands (using your fingers, of course). People make all kinds of things with their hands, although sometimes, that's not so easy to do!

And what about your feet—the parts of you that carry you around all day? Every time you take a step, your toes make a little grab at the ground and keep you from falling. Some people can even pick up things with their toes, but you may have noticed that hands are much better for that.

Aren't you glad you have teeth to chew your food with?
If you couldn't use your teeth to chew your food, your poor
stomach wouldn't be able to digest all those big lumps.
  Your first set of teeth are called your baby teeth. When
you are about six years old, these teeth begin to fall out.
Underneath your baby teeth is a whole set of other
teeth—your grown-up teeth. Take good care of these teeth;
they have to last you the rest of your life.

Teeth are bones covered with enamel. That makes them very hard. But sometimes your teeth get little holes in them, called cavities. This may happen when you don't brush them. The old food stays on your teeth, making the enamel wear away or decay. The dentist can clean your teeth and fill the cavities.

Inside your head is a very important part of you called your brain. All your thinking is done there. But your brain does much more than help you think. It takes care of you in other ways, even though you may not know that anything is happening. Your brain keeps your heart beating, your stomach digesting, and your lungs breathing in and out all the time. Your brain never sleeps, although parts of it do rest while you sleep.

Your brain is also like a big closet. It stores up everything you do and learn, so that you can remember it all later.

You have some very important helpers called your senses. You have five senses—sight, hearing, smell, taste, and touch.

You see with your eyes. You can see things up close, like flowers and bugs, and you can see things far away, like clouds and stars.

Your eye is like a little round camera that makes a picture of what you see and sends it to your brain. When your eyes are open, the light that bounces off things goes into your eyes and makes the picture. When your eyes are closed, there is no light shining into them, and you can't see.

You hear with your ears. When something makes a
noise, it sends waves of sound through the air. These waves
make your eardrums quiver—the way the top of a drum
quivers when you hit it.

Sometimes, things make such loud noises that you have
to put your hands over your ears. Or sometimes, you have to
listen very carefully to find out what is going on.

Your nose is good for two things. You breathe in and out through your nose, and you smell things with your nose. When air goes into your nose, your nose picks up all the different smells that are around you—like flowers or delicious food.

Your sense of smell also helps you enjoy the food you are eating. Nothing tastes good when you have a cold because you can't smell when your nose is stuffed up.

You taste things with your tongue. Your tongue is covered with tiny bumps called taste buds. The taste buds on different parts of your tongue help you recognize different tastes. The front ones taste sweet things and salty things. The side ones taste sour things like lemons and pickles. The back ones taste bitter things.

Touch is another one of your senses. When your skin touches something, you can tell many things about it. It might be wet. It might be dry. It might be rough, or it might be smooth. Some things are hot, and some are cold. And some are soft or hard or sharp.

If you pet a cat, you can feel how soft and smooth it is. If you pick up a stone, you can tell whether it is dry or wet or rough or smooth. You can also tell the shape of something when you feel it with your hands.

LUNCH
SNACK SNACK
SNACK SNACK
SNACK SNACK
BREAKFAST SNACK
SNACK SNACK
DINNER

When your body needs something, it lets you know. When you are hungry, your stomach growls. It is saying, "Feed me." If you never felt hungry, you would probably forget to eat.

When you need water, you feel thirsty. Then you run to get a glass of water.

When you are cold, your skin gets little goose bumps, and you start to shiver. That warms you up. You also put your thick sweater on.

Because you have so many things to do all day, you get very tired. That's why you feel sleepy at night. Everyone needs sleep. Since you are young and still growing, you need even more sleep than your mother and father. Growing takes a lot of energy. While you are asleep, your heart keeps beating and your lungs keep breathing. You are also busy having dreams.

Your body has special ways to let you know if things are not all right inside. One way is pain. You probably wish you didn't have to feel hurt, but pain is a way of telling you that you need to take care of something. Otherwise, you might not know that anything is wrong. If your eye hurts, the pain may be telling you that something is in your eye. If your shoes are uncomfortable, your feet begin to hurt. Your feet are telling you, "Take those off!" So you do.

Sometimes, you don't feel well. You may even have a fever. Then your mother takes your temperature and sends you to bed. A fever is one way that your body has to fight off germs. If you rest, you can use all your energy to fight those germs—and win.

Sometimes, you are so sick you have to see a doctor. But a doctor isn't someone you see only if you are sick. When you go to the doctor and have a checkup, the doctor weighs you and measures you to see how much you've grown since the last visit. The doctor checks your ears, looks down your throat, and looks into your eyes.

The doctor might also give you an injection. Some people call it a "shot." It feels like a very short, big pinch. Injections help your body fight off germs. They do hurt a little, but being sick feels worse and lasts much longer than a little injection.

People have other kinds of feelings besides feeling sick or sleepy or hungry. Often you feel happy. And sometimes you feel angry or sad or lonely or frightened.

Everyone has these feelings inside them at one time or another. They are part of what makes you yourself.

Sometimes you get angry when you make a mistake. Other times you are sad because something is wrong, or you don't understand something. Even your friends may not understand how bad you feel. But if you talk to someone, often that person can make you feel better. This is one way that people help each other.

At the end of the day,
it's time to brush your teeth,
wash your face, comb your hair

—and get ready for bed. After all, your body needs plenty of rest to do some exciting things tomorrow. And the more good things you do for yourself, the more good things *you* can do.

PEOPLE AT WORK

It's morning and everyone is getting up.
Everywhere people are getting ready to do their jobs.
All the different jobs people do are important, because
almost everything we eat, wear, use, live in, or enjoy is
made somewhere by someone.

Some people have jobs in factories or stores or office buildings. Some people work at home. Some people have jobs helping other people.

It might be snowing.

It might be raining.

But most people get to their jobs no matter what.

There's a fire on Tenth Street!
The fire fighters slide down the
pole and jump onto the fire trucks.

Ding! Ding! Out of the way!
Here's the fire. Get out the hoses!

It was just a pot roast burning. Nothing serious.

Back to the fire station to get the trucks ready for the next alarm.

Doctors and nurses take care of people when they are sick.
They also help people take care of themselves when they are healthy.
Huey, Dewey, and Louie are getting their checkups. The doctor
looks down Dewey's throat. He weighs and measures Huey, and he
gives Louie a shot to help him stay healthy.

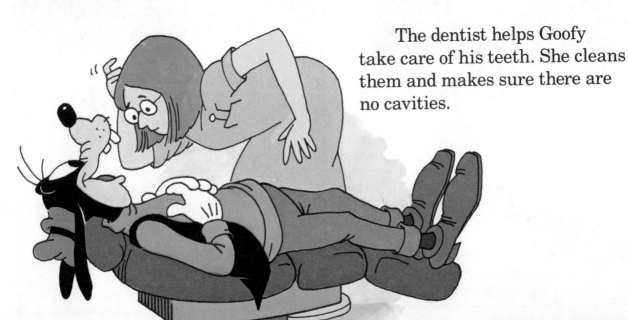

The dentist helps Goofy
take care of his teeth. She cleans
them and makes sure there are
no cavities.

Sometimes, people get sick and have to go to the hospital.
All kinds of people work in a hospital. There are doctors and nurses
and X-ray technicians and nurse's aides and ambulance drivers.
These people all help make sure that the patients get well.

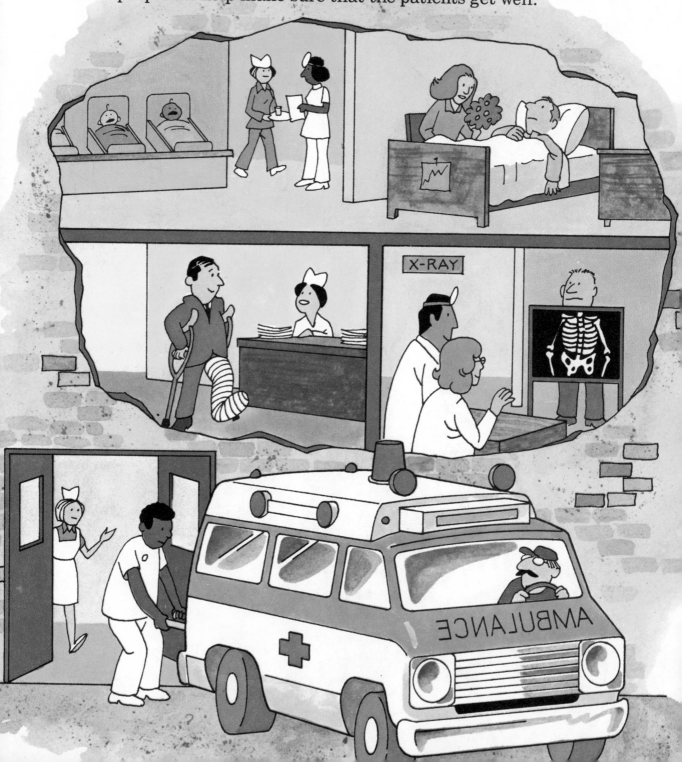

Police officers help people in many different ways.
Chief O'Hara patrols the streets to keep them safe.

He directs traffic and makes sure that everyone crosses the street safely.

Morty and Ferdie are going
to the library because they want
to borrow some books. The
librarian helps Morty find a book
about animals. Ferdie wants
a book of riddles.

Houses and apartments are built by people called builders. These builders are building a new house for Minnie. First the workers dig a big hole, and then they pour in the concrete to make the foundation. Trucks take away all the dirt and bring back the wood the builders will need to make the walls.

Then a bricklayer builds the chimney, the roofer puts the shingles on the roof, the carpenters put up the walls and put in the windows and doors, the plumber puts in all the pipes, and the electrician puts in all the wires. The paperhanger and the painter come to put up the wallpaper and paint the rooms. Minnie chooses the colors she wants in her living room.

All the things we use are made somewhere by someone. People who work in factories make the clothes we buy in the store.

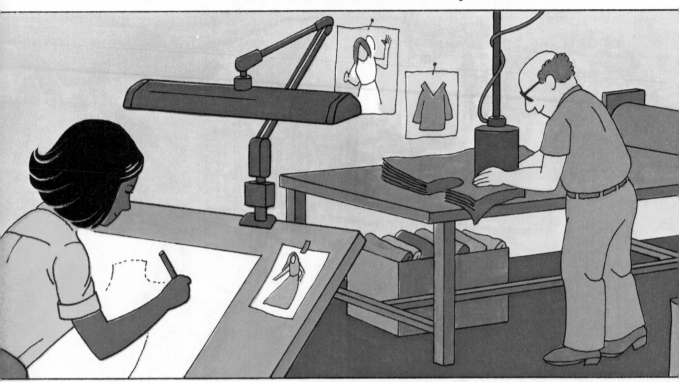

A designer makes the pattern, a cutter cuts out the material, and a sewer sews all the pieces together.

In a car factory, the workers put together the cars on a long, moving assembly line.

They put the body of the car together. Then they put in the motor and put on the wheels. The finished car is driven off the assembly line. Donald can hardly wait to buy one!

When something you buy breaks, someone has to fix it. The worker who works in the repair shop can fix that toaster for Donald.

The washing machine repairman comes and fixes the washing machine right in Donald's house.

When the pipes in Goofy's house leak, the plumber stops the water from spilling all over Goofy's kitchen.

The gas station is a kind of repair shop, too. The garage mechanics fix your car, change the oil or the tires, or "fill 'er up" with gasoline. A truck driver delivers the gasoline that you buy at the gas station.

GAS

Some people drive cars when they want to go somewhere.
But sometimes, it's easier to take a bus, a taxicab, a train,
or a plane.

Goofy is going to take the bus. He pays his fare to the bus driver.
Donald is late. He is going to take a taxi.

Mickey is going on a train trip. He buys his ticket from the ticket clerk and gets on the train. The engineer drives the engine that pulls the train cars into the station.

When Mickey finds a seat, the conductor comes and punches his ticket. The conductor calls out the names of the different stations so that people will know when to get off.

Donald is taking Huey on an airplane trip to visit Uncle Scrooge. Many different people work at the airport. They help the passengers get safely and comfortably to the right places—with all their luggage.

Donald buys the tickets from the ticket clerk and gets the luggage weighed.

Then the baggage clerk puts the suitcases on a truck.

The baggage handler loads the baggage on the plane.

Food is loaded onto the plane, too. The flight attendant welcomes everyone on bo

The pilot prepares to take off. "Fasten your seat belts, please."
The flight attendant serves Donald and Huey their lunch.

The farmer grows vegetables in the fields. You can see lettuce and string beans and tomatoes and corn.

The farmer harvests wheat for bread.

Apples and pears have to be picked.

The milk we drink comes from cows.

Chickens lay the eggs we eat for breakfast.

And all this food is driven to the market and to places where some foods are put in special packages.

In a frozen-food factory, the fresh meat, fish, and vegetables are put in packages and frozen before they go to the store.

Some foods are cooked and put in cans. This way, they will stay fresh for a long time.

Some foods, like breakfast cereals, are mixed in the factory. On their class trip, Morty and Ferdie see the cereal go into boxes.

Truck drivers deliver the packages, cans, and boxes to stores in every neighborhood.

Daisy goes shopping in a supermarket that sells all kinds of food. Truck drivers deliver food from the farms and the food factories. People who work in the store unload it and put it on the shelves. Daisy picks out the foods she wants. Then she will pay the cashier, who works in the front of the store.

Some stores sell special things, or things that were made right in the store.

The baker makes cakes and breads and cookies at the bakery.

The toy store owner sells toys, and sometimes makes them, too.

The pharmacist in the drugstore mixes the medicines so they are ready to sell.

Mail is very important. Many people work together to make sure that all the letters and packages get to the right places.

Huey, Dewey, and Louie are writing a letter to Grandma Duck.

The mail carrier picks up the letter from the mailbox and takes it to the post office.

The mail sorters sort the letters. They make sure that Grandma's letter is sent to the right town.

A truck driver drives the mailbags to the post office in Grandma's town.

There, Grandma Duck's mail carrier delivers the letter right to her mailbox.

"What a nice letter!"

Books tell us all kinds of important things. They show us how the world works, and they help us enjoy our quiet times.
Writers write the books.

The people who work at the printers use big presses on which the pages of the book are printed.
The binders put the pages together to make up the book you buy in the store.

At school the teacher is teaching Huey, Dewey, and Louie how to read books. Dewey likes storybooks. Huey likes books about animals. They have fun learning how to count and how to write letters on the blackboard.

Huey, Dewey, and Louie enjoy going to school because their teacher tells them so many exciting things. Today, Huey is finding out all about lions.

Some people entertain us. Actors and dancers and singers make us feel happy.

Some entertainers make television shows. Lots of people work at the television studio.

The person with the camera takes a moving picture of the people in the television show.

Then the show is broadcast from the television station. If you turn on your television set, you can watch the show at home.

Some people make beautiful things for us to look at. They are called artists.

Painters paint pictures.

Sculptors make statues.

People like to go to museums and look at all the beautiful things artists have been busy making.

Many people have jobs making energy to run all the machines and appliances we use. We can get energy from coal, oil, the wind, and the sun.

Coal miners are the people who dig coal. Truck drivers take the coal to the generating plant. There the coal is burned to make steam. The big generators turn this steam into electricity.

In our homes we need electricity to light the lights
and run the refrigerator, the toaster, the record player—
and many other things, too.

At the end of the day, when all the work is done, it is time to clean up. Every day, people throw out garbage. The sanitation worker will come early the next morning to take it away.

In the house it's time to clean up, too. Morty and Ferdie
help Mickey after a long day.

Everyone has a job and every job is important. Children
have jobs that are important, too. Everybody helps
everybody else. That's what makes life so interesting and so
much fun.